KU-572-083

Withdrawn from Stock
Dublin City Public Libraries

HEALTH MATTERS

UNDERSTANDING ALLERGIES

BY
HOLLY DUHIG

BookLife
PUBLISHING

©2018
BookLife Publishing
King's Lynn
Norfolk PE30 4LS

Printed in Malaysia.

A catalogue record for this book is available from the British Library.

ISBN: 978-1-78637-338-0

Written by:
Holly Duhig

Edited by:
John Wood

Designed by:
Drue Rintoul

CONTENTS

Words that look like **this** are explained in the glossary on page 31.

ALLERGIES

If you have ever had the sniffles on a summer's day or needed to sneeze after stroking your friend's cat, then you might suffer from an allergy.

There are lots of things people can be allergic to. A **substance** that can cause allergies is known as an allergen. Common food allergens include peanuts, eggs and shellfish. Some medicines, such as penicillin, can be allergens. So can some metals, such as nickel.

SOME KEYS ARE MADE FROM NICKEL.

PENICILLIN IS A TYPE OF MOULD USED AS A MEDICINE.

FACT

ALLERGIES ARE VERY COMMON; THEY AFFECT 30 PERCENT OF ADULTS AND 40 PERCENT OF CHILDREN.

Symptoms

An allergy is an unusual bodily response to something which, to most people, is harmless. Because of this, coming into contact with an allergen might cause you to have **symptoms** such as itchy skin, a runny nose or watery eyes. These symptoms are part of an allergic reaction.

If you have an allergy, you might need to see a doctor about your symptoms. Doctors can help by teaching you how to keep away from the thing you are allergic to, or by giving you medicine to help lessen the symptoms.

FACT

MEDICINES THAT HELP WITH ALLERGIES ARE OFTEN CALLED ANTIHISTAMINES.

WHY DO WE GET ALLERGIES?

The Immune System

We get allergies because of our immune systems. Our bodies have lots of systems that keep us alive and healthy, including a nervous system which sends signals and information around the body, a circulatory system which pumps blood around the body and a digestive system which breaks down food and fuels your body. Your immune system, however, is the system that protects your body from sickness and disease.

FACT

IF YOUR BODY WAS A COUNTRY, YOUR IMMUNE SYSTEM WOULD BE ITS ARMY, FIGHTING OFF NASTY INVADERS CALLED PATHOGENS.

Pathogens such as germs, bacteria or viruses, can cause us to become ill. Your immune system sends white blood **cells** to help fight off these pathogens. The symptoms of an allergic reaction, such as a runny nose, rash, sickness or diarrhoea, can be very similar to the symptoms of a disease, like a cold or the flu. This is because your body reacts to the **microscopic particles** in an allergen, such as a peanut, in the same way that it would react to a flu-causing pathogen.

WHITE BLOOD CELL

FACT

WHEN THE IMMUNE SYSTEM TRIES TO FIGHT OFF SOMETHING THAT ISN'T A PATHOGEN – LIKE TREE POLLEN OR CAT HAIR – WE GET AN ALLERGIC REACTION.

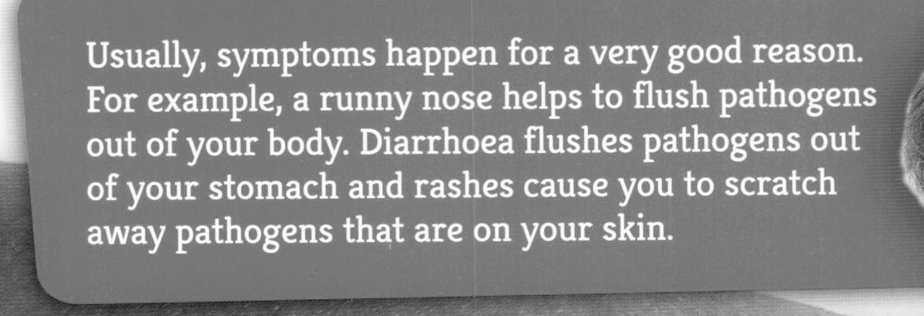

Usually, symptoms happen for a very good reason. For example, a runny nose helps to flush pathogens out of your body. Diarrhoea flushes pathogens out of your stomach and rashes cause you to scratch away pathogens that are on your skin.

RASH

Entry Points

Allergens enter your body in the same ways that germs and bacteria do – through your nose, lungs, mouth, stomach or even through a cut in your skin. These places are called entry points. Some allergens, like pollen, enter your body through your nose, while other allergens, like those found in foods, enter through your mouth.

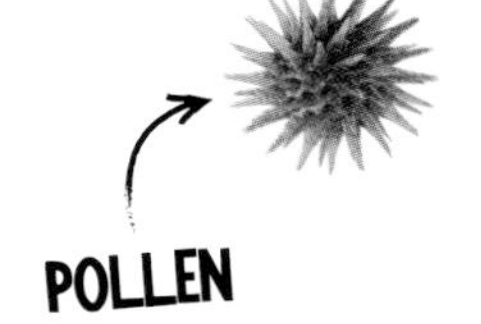

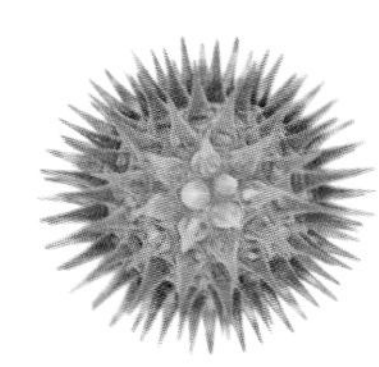

POLLEN

Entry points are very useful. We need them for all sorts of important things such as eating and breathing. However, they also make our bodies very **vulnerable**. Because of this, these places in your body are packed full of cells called mast cells, which help fight off nasty invaders.

If your immune system is your body's army, then white blood cells and mast cells are its soldiers. They release **chemicals**, called histamines, to fight off invaders. Mast cells in your nose release histamines that make your nose run. Histamines in your stomach cause sickness and diarrhoea, while histamines on your skin make your skin itch.

HAY FEVER

Some people are allergic to pollen, which is the fine, powdery substance made by plants. This is called allergic rhinitis but it is more commonly known as hay fever. Hay fever happens when the body thinks pollen is a harmful invader and tries to fight it off.

Where Does Pollen Come From?

Most plants and flowers have both male and female parts. Pollen is made by the male part of a plant and is carried to the female part of another plant. This is called pollination. Pollen is carried by the wind, or by insects such as bees and butterflies.

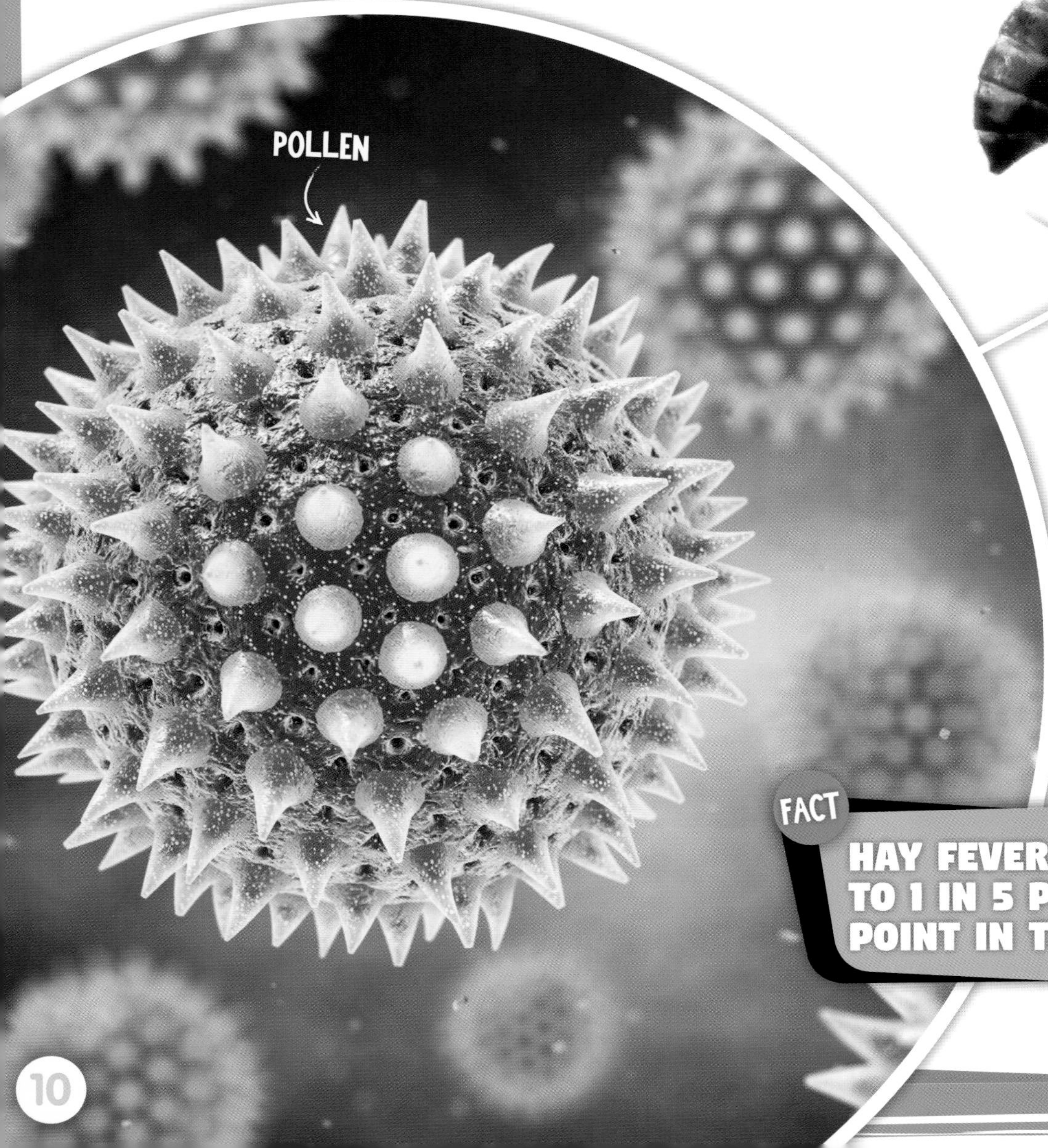

POLLEN

FACT

HAY FEVER WILL AFFECT UP TO 1 IN 5 PEOPLE AT SOME POINT IN THEIR LIVES.

Hay fever is seasonal, which means it affects people at certain times of the year. People who are allergic to tree pollen tend to get hay fever in spring because that's when trees pollinate. People who are allergic to grass pollen get symptoms in summer.

Hay fever can cause a person to get itchy, watery eyes and a runny nose. It can feel a lot like having a cold. Luckily, many people only have hay fever when they are young and grow out of it by the time they reach adulthood.

FACT

AROUND 95% OF HAY FEVER SUFFERERS ARE ALLERGIC TO GRASS POLLEN.

The Body's Response

When a person with hay fever breathes in pollen, their immune system reacts by releasing antibodies. Antibodies are made by white blood cells and are very helpful in fighting off harmful invaders. They are shaped in a certain way so they can attach themselves to the pollen particles and **ingest** them. You can think of it like a lock and key, or two puzzle pieces.

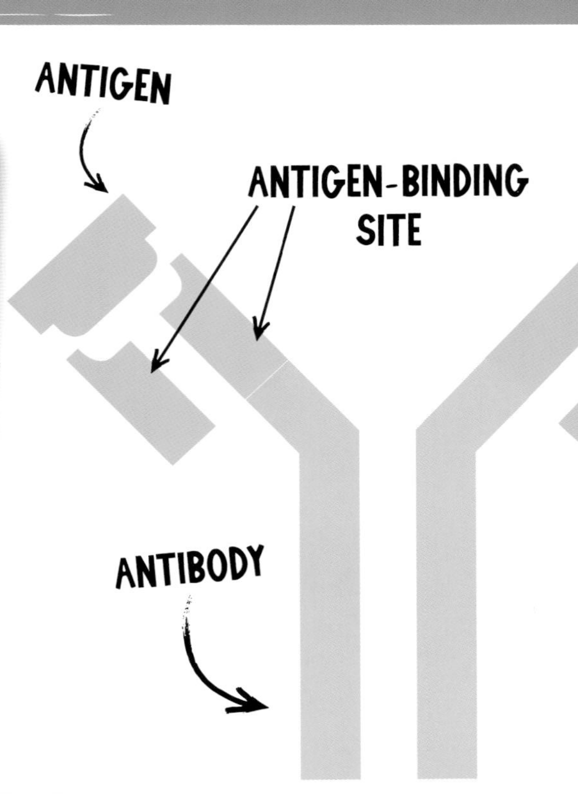

When this happens, mast cells release histamines. These histamines then tell cells in your throat and nose to **swell** up and release **fluid**. This causes common hay fever symptoms such as blocked or runny noses.

Treating Hay Fever

Hay fever symptoms can be uncomfortable, but they can be treated using medicines, called anti-histamines, which stop histamines from working so they can't tell cells to release fluid.

FACT

NASAL SPRAYS AND EYE DROPS CAN ALSO HELP TREAT HAY FEVER.

TOP TIPS FOR DEALING WITH HAY FEVER

- WEAR SUNGLASSES AS MUCH AS POSSIBLE. THIS STOPS POLLEN IN THE AIR FROM GETTING INTO YOUR EYES.
- KEEP BEDROOM WINDOWS CLOSED AT NIGHT AND CAR WINDOWS CLOSED WHILE TRAVELLING.
- APPLY PETROLEUM JELLY TO THE SKIN AROUND YOUR EYES AND NOSE. THIS HELPS BECAUSE THE POLLEN WILL STICK TO THE JELLY BEFORE IT REACHES YOUR NOSE AND EYES.
- WASH YOUR FACE BEFORE AND AFTER PLAYING OUTSIDE.

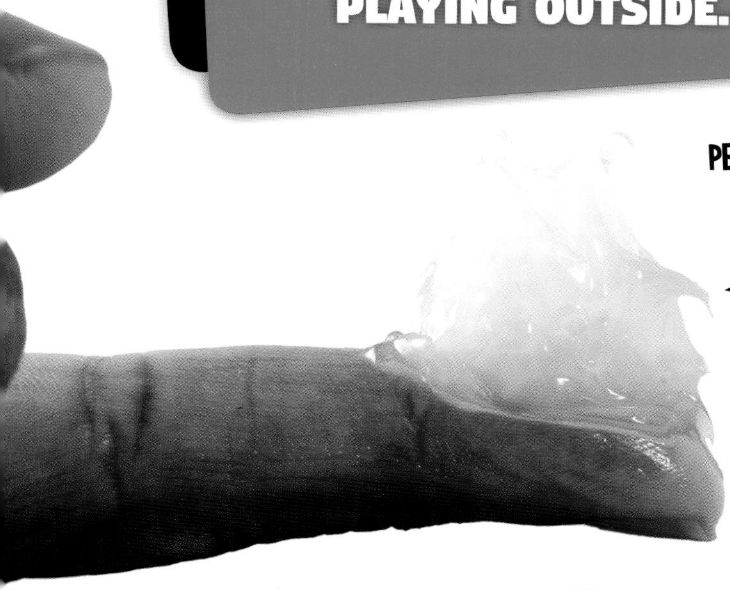

PETROLEUM JELLY

NASAL SPRAY

FOOD ALLERGIES

Lots of people have food allergies. It is thought that food allergies affect around 220 to 250 million people in the world. Some of the most common food allergies are:

Food allergies are often **inherited**. This means that if parents have an allergy to a certain type of food, they are likely to pass it on to their children. Food allergies happen when someone is allergic to the **proteins** in certain foods.

Allergy or Intolerance?

As well as allergies, lots of people have food intolerances. You are said to have a food intolerance when your body finds it difficult to **digest** a certain type of food. Food intolerances are different to allergies because it is your digestive system, rather than your immune system, that is reacting to the food.

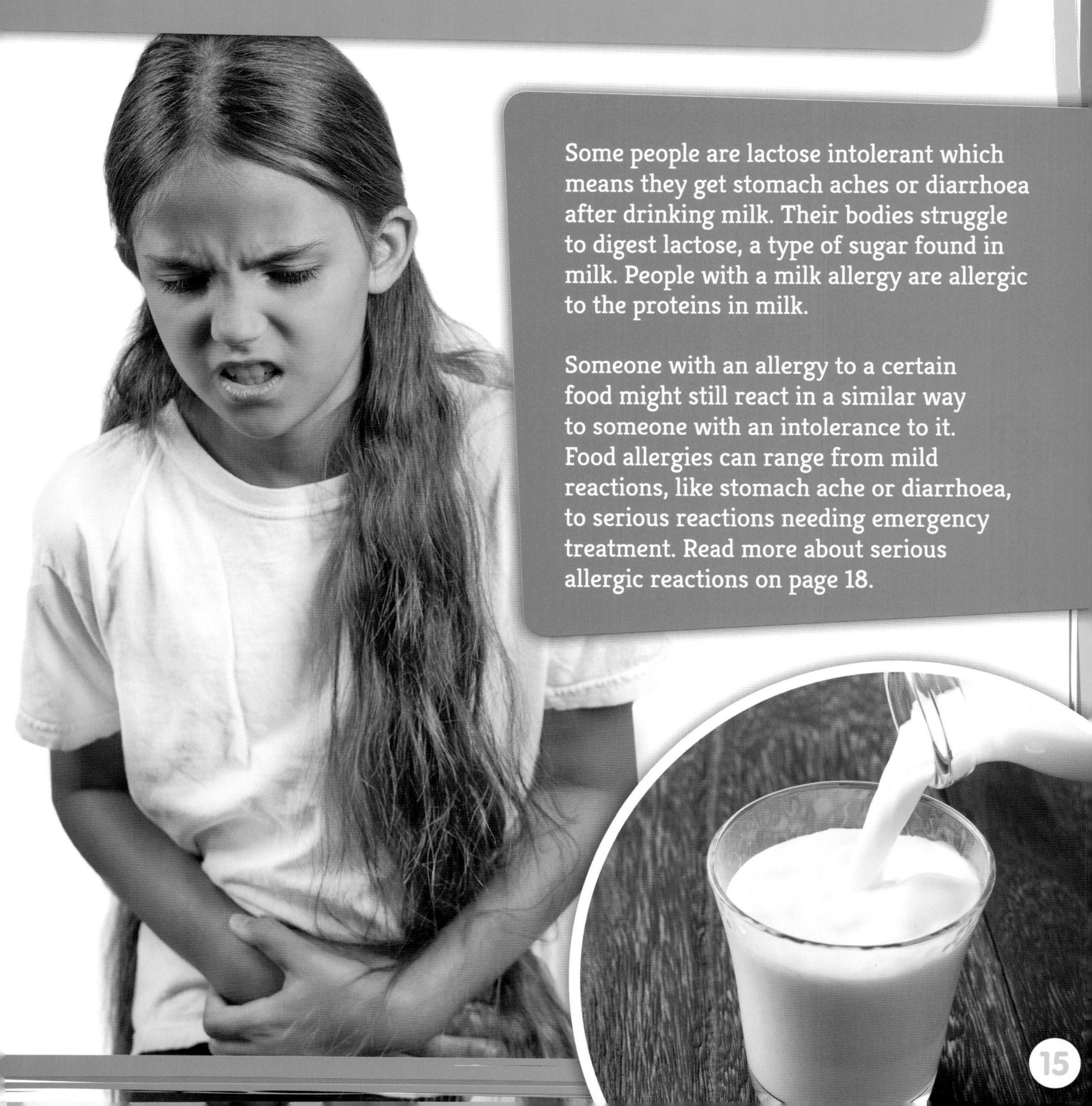

Some people are lactose intolerant which means they get stomach aches or diarrhoea after drinking milk. Their bodies struggle to digest lactose, a type of sugar found in milk. People with a milk allergy are allergic to the proteins in milk.

Someone with an allergy to a certain food might still react in a similar way to someone with an intolerance to it. Food allergies can range from mild reactions, like stomach ache or diarrhoea, to serious reactions needing emergency treatment. Read more about serious allergic reactions on page 18.

TREATING FOOD ALLERGIES

There is no cure for food allergies. While we can treat the symptoms of an allergic reaction, there is no way of stopping our bodies from reacting to certain allergens. One of the most common food allergies is an allergy to peanuts. Peanut allergies can be especially dangerous because the proteins in peanuts can get into your blood before they are fully destroyed by your stomach.

FACT

PEANUTS AREN'T ACTUALLY NUTS. THEY ARE IN FACT A TYPE OF LEGUME!

Reading Labels

The main way to treat food allergies is to learn how to stay away from the type of food you are allergic to. On food packaging, there should always be a label with a list of ingredients. This is very useful for people with allergies.

LABELS LIKE THIS LET PEOPLE KNOW WHEN FOOD CONTAINS AN ALLERGEN.

However, these labels can sometimes be hard to read. If you are worried that a snack contains something that you are allergic to, always ask an adult to check the label first. They will know how to read the ingredients list and check for allergens.

ANAPHYLACTIC SHOCK

Some allergic reactions can be small, while others can be much more **severe**. Severe allergic reactions can lead to something called an anaphylactic shock (say 'anna-fill-ak-tick' shock). This is when the immune system reacts so strongly that it harms the body instead of protecting it. If an anaphylactic shock isn't treated straight away, it can cause someone to die.

Because of this, it is important to be able to recognise the symptoms of an anaphylactic shock. People suffering from anaphylactic shock might have:

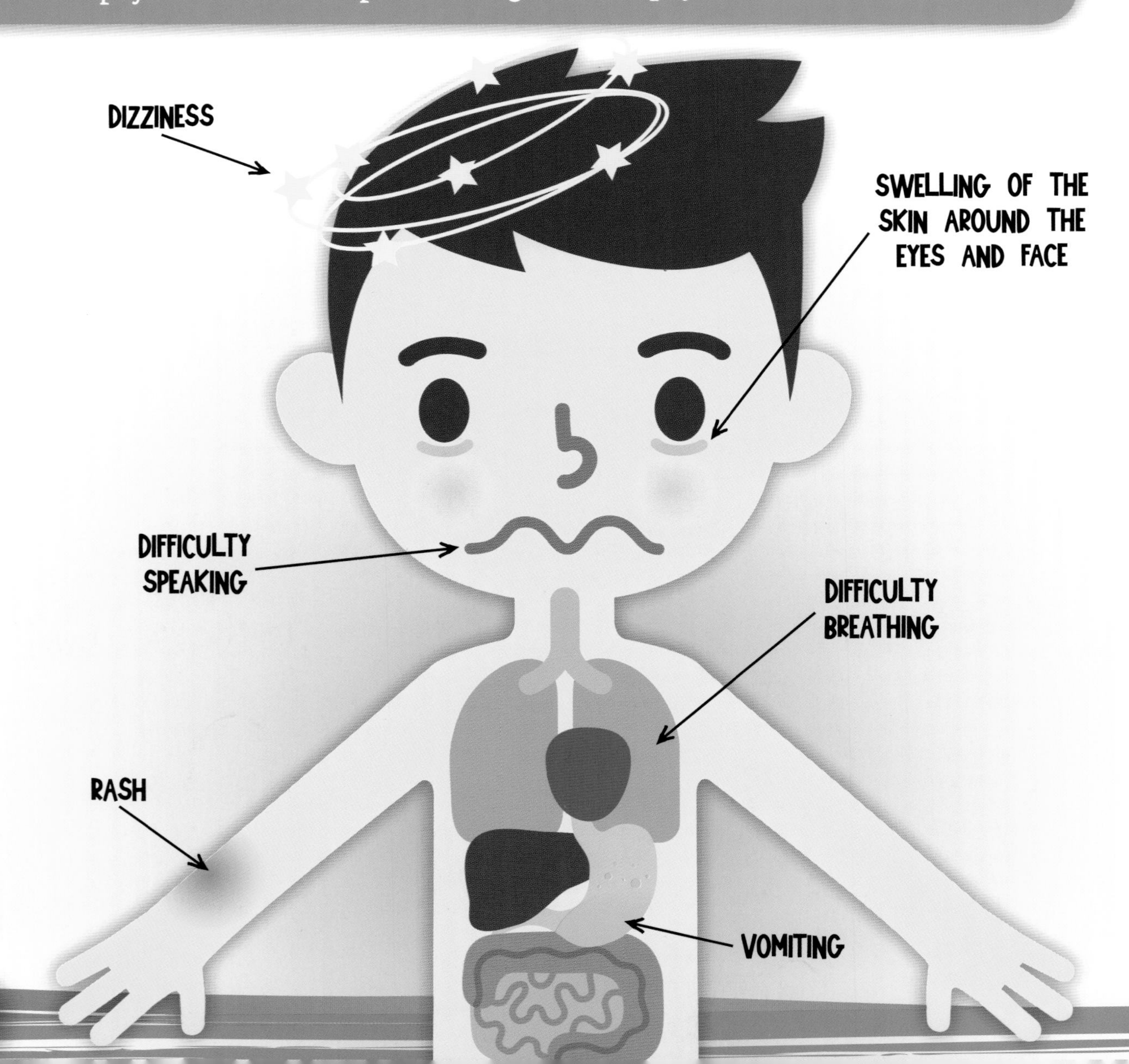

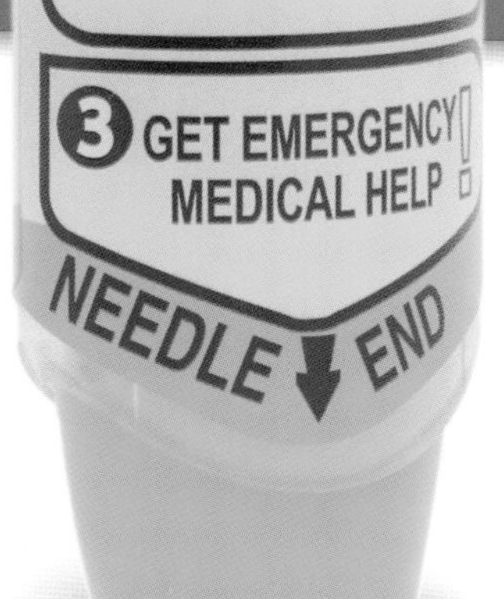

EPIPEN WITH INSTRUCTIONS

What to Do

If you think someone is having an anaphylactic shock, you should let an adult know straight away so they can call the emergency services. If there are no adults around, you can call the emergency services yourself.

FACT

IT IS IMPORTANT TO KNOW THE NUMBER FOR THE EMERGENCY SERVICES WHERE YOU LIVE. YOU NEVER KNOW WHEN YOU MIGHT NEED IT.

Most people who suffer from severe allergies carry an EpiPen, which is a type of medicine that someone can inject themselves with if they start having an anaphylactic shock. EpiPens have instructions on the side. These show other people how to use the medicine if the person having the shock is not able to speak.

How Do EpiPens Work?

EpiPens work by injecting adrenaline, which is also called epinephrine (say 'eppy-NEF-rin'). You might not have heard of adrenaline but you will have felt it. Have you ever had a racing heart and jelly legs before doing something scary like riding a rollercoaster or taking a test? Those feelings are caused by adrenaline – a natural **hormone** that is released when you are stressed. In an emergency, EpiPens can be injected into someone's thigh and adrenaline will be released.

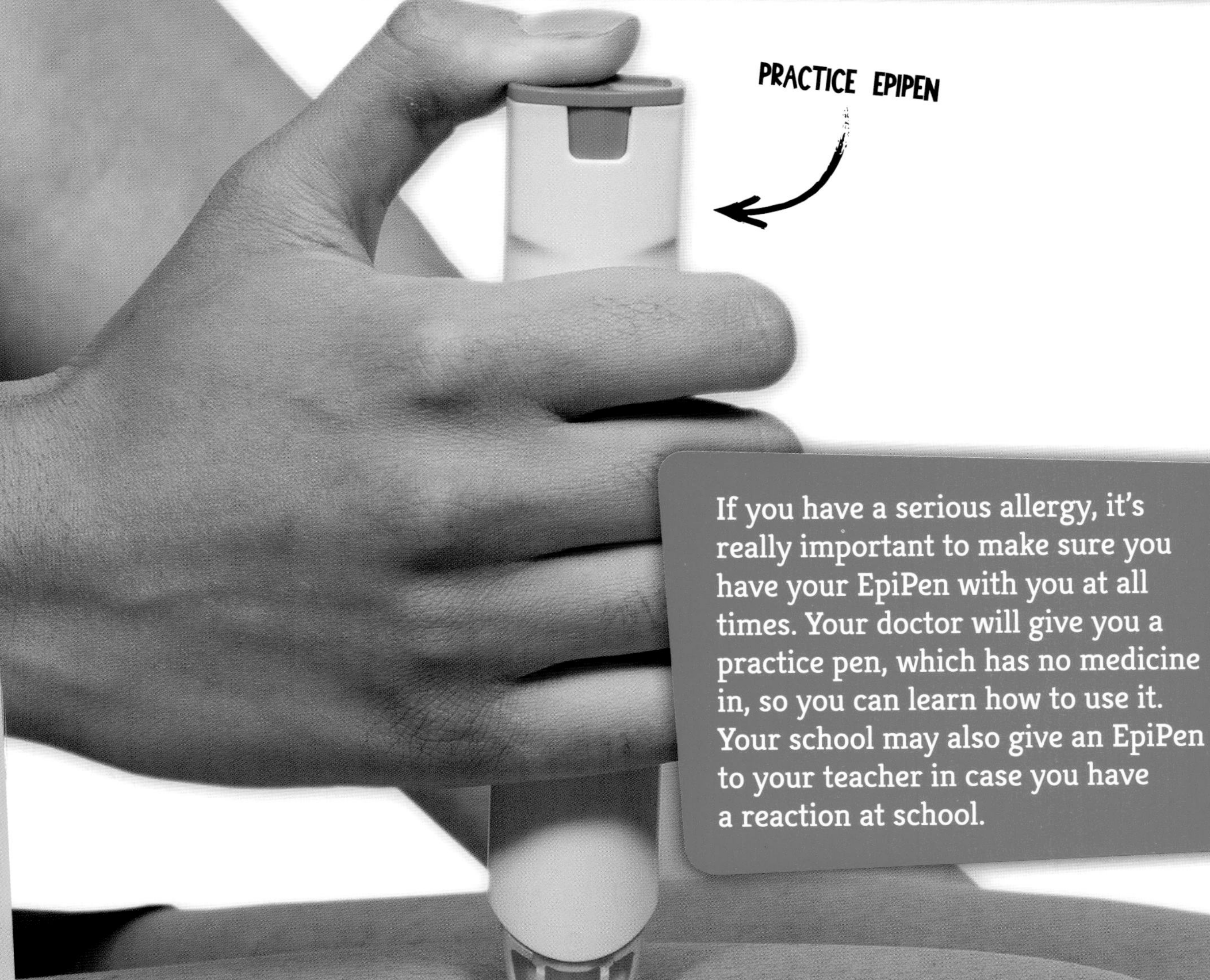

If you have a serious allergy, it's really important to make sure you have your EpiPen with you at all times. Your doctor will give you a practice pen, which has no medicine in, so you can learn how to use it. Your school may also give an EpiPen to your teacher in case you have a reaction at school.

When someone is having an anaphylactic shock, their **blood pressure** drops. This means less blood is reaching important parts of the body, like the brain, which can cause dizziness. The adrenaline in an EpiPen **constricts** a person's blood vessels, which causes their blood pressure to go back to normal. It also lessens swelling and itching, and opens the airways so the person can breathe normally again.

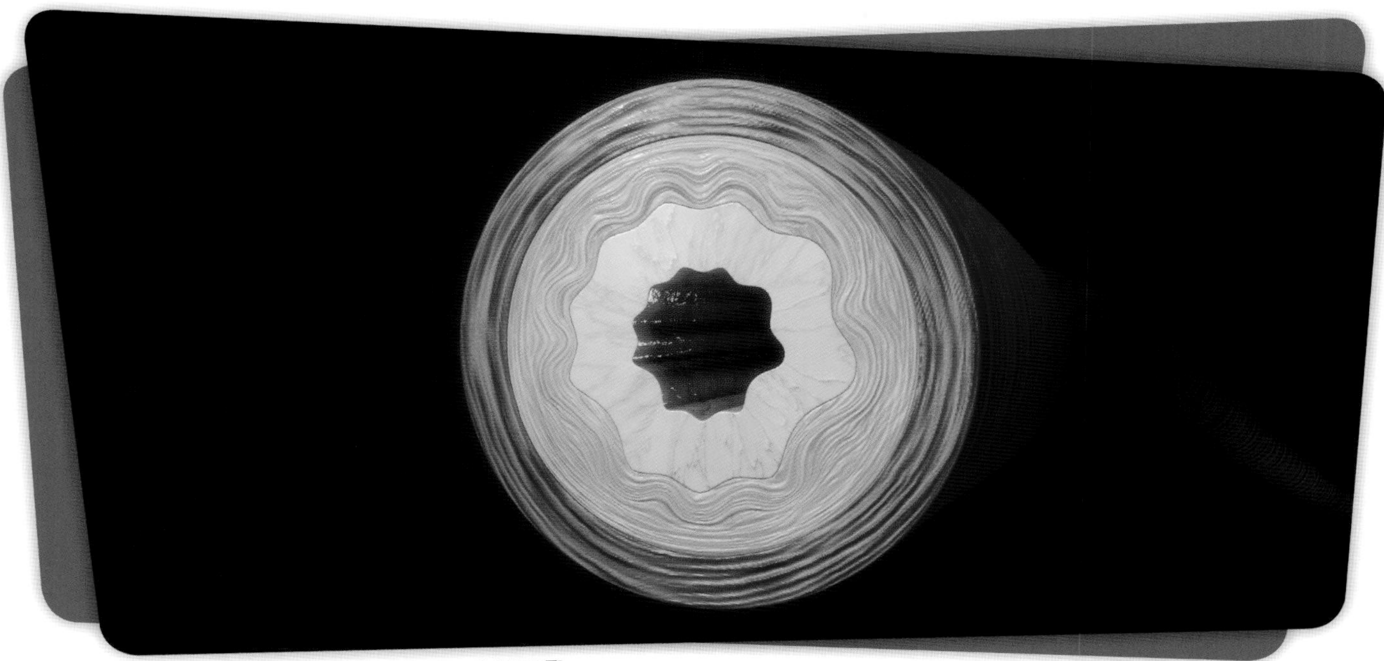

CONSTRICTED BLOOD VESSEL

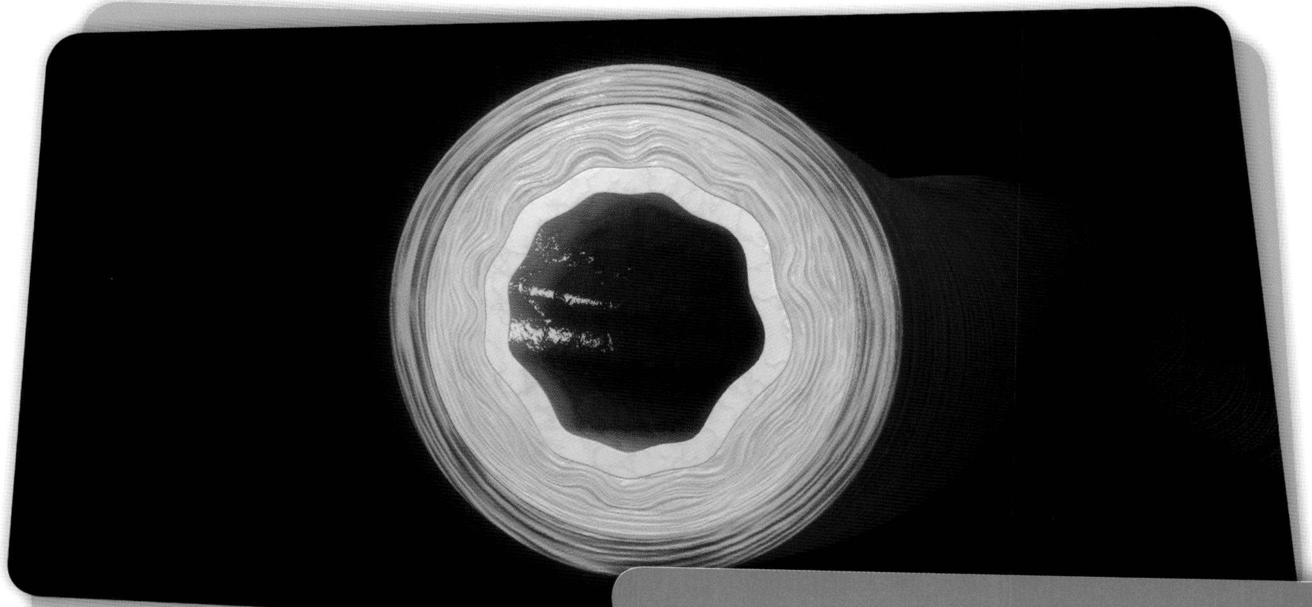

NORMAL BLOOD VESSEL

Children with severe allergies might wear a wristband. This lets other people know what they are allergic to so they can help them avoid certain allergens.

CASE STUDY: JASMINE

Meet Jasmine. She is allergic to the **venom** in bee stings. Let's find out more about how she manages her allergy.

Hello, I'm Jasmine. I found out I was allergic to bees when I accidently stood on a bee while playing in the park without any shoes on. It stung me and my skin started swelling up really fast. Soon, I felt really dizzy and couldn't breathe properly. My aunt took me to the hospital where they gave me an injection to stop the reaction.

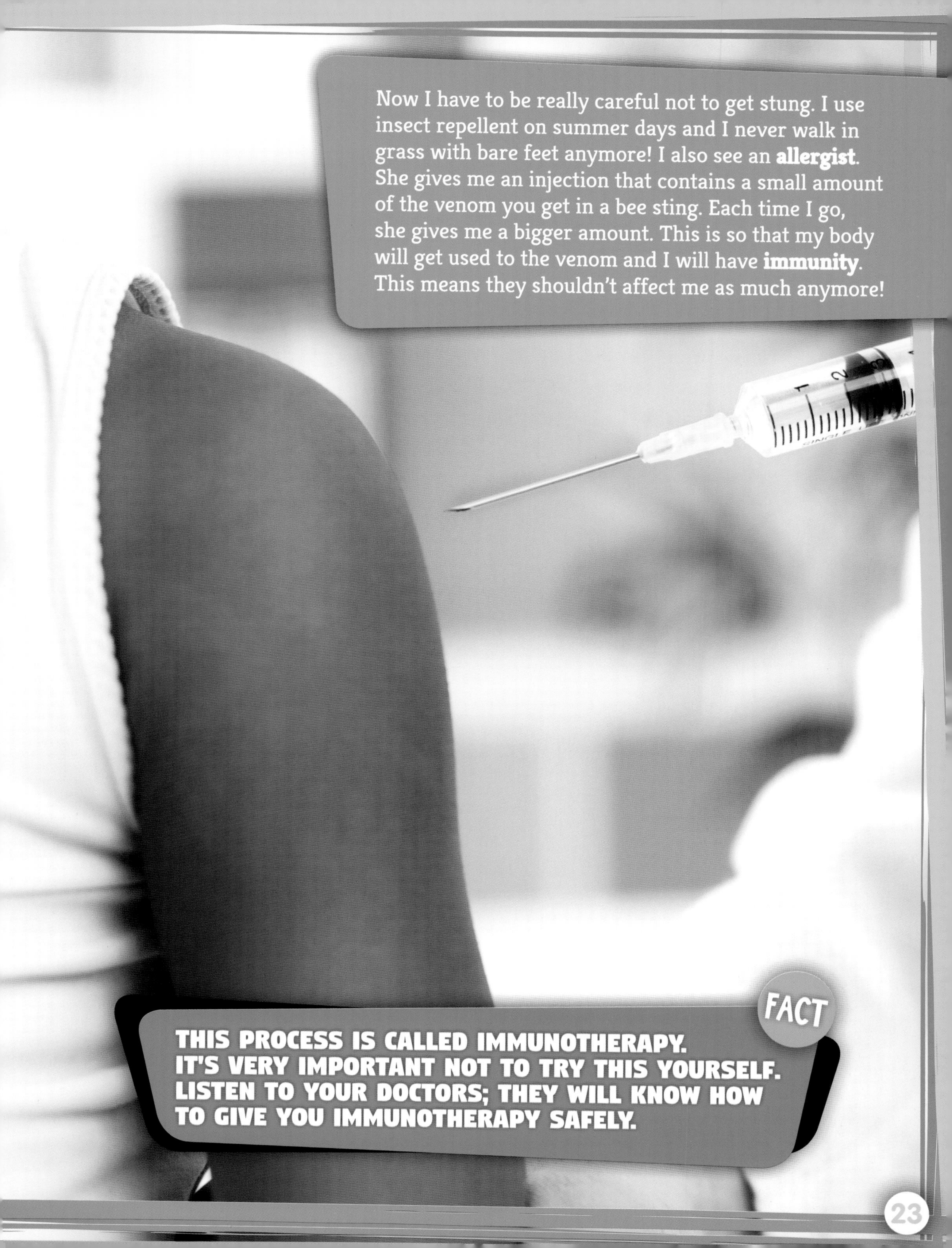

Now I have to be really careful not to get stung. I use insect repellent on summer days and I never walk in grass with bare feet anymore! I also see an **allergist**. She gives me an injection that contains a small amount of the venom you get in a bee sting. Each time I go, she gives me a bigger amount. This is so that my body will get used to the venom and I will have **immunity**. This means they shouldn't affect me as much anymore!

FACT

THIS PROCESS IS CALLED IMMUNOTHERAPY. IT'S VERY IMPORTANT NOT TO TRY THIS YOURSELF. LISTEN TO YOUR DOCTORS; THEY WILL KNOW HOW TO GIVE YOU IMMUNOTHERAPY SAFELY.

ASTHMA AND ALLERGIES

Asthma is a health condition that affects the lungs and makes it difficult to breathe. Asthma is caused by the swelling of the airways that carry air to the lungs. This swelling causes the airways to become much tighter and become clogged with **mucus**.

NORMAL AIRWAY

ASTHMATIC AIRWAY

ASTHMA ATTACK

WALL INFLAMED AND THICKENED

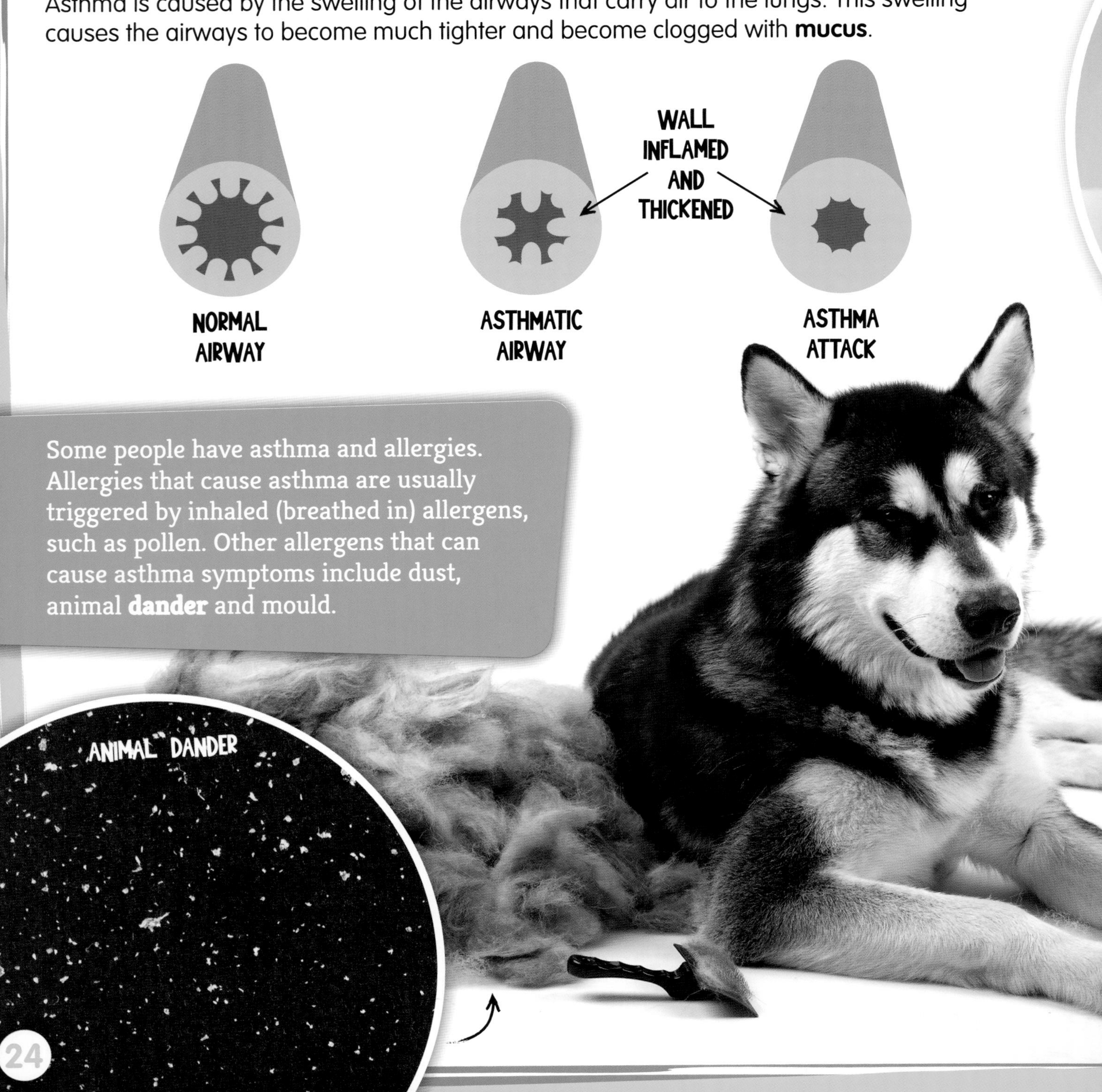

Some people have asthma and allergies. Allergies that cause asthma are usually triggered by inhaled (breathed in) allergens, such as pollen. Other allergens that can cause asthma symptoms include dust, animal **dander** and mould.

When asthma symptoms get suddenly worse it is called an asthma attack. Asthma attacks can be frightening but luckily there are lots of treatments.

Asthma symptoms can be treated using inhalers. Inhalers contain medicine that can be breathed in. This medicine relaxes the muscles in the airways and allows the sufferer to breathe easily again. People with asthma that is triggered by allergies can also take antihistamine medicines. This makes an asthma attack less likely to happen in the first place.

CASE STUDY: MADELINE

Meet Madeline. She suffers from allergies and asthma. Let's see how she manages them day-to-day.

Hi! My name is Madeline. I am allergic to dust, dust mites and pollen. Breathing in too much dust or pollen sets off my asthma and makes me very wheezy. This means my lungs tighten up and make a whistling sound. It's very uncomfortable. We don't have carpets in our house because they collect too much dust. Instead we have wooden floors and my dad vacuums them when it gets too dusty! My bed has a mite-proof cover to stop dust mites that live in the mattress from making me cough.

MITE-PROOF COVER

DUST MITES ARE TINY CREATURES THAT LIVE IN HOUSE DUST AND LINEN.

During the summer, my hay fever flares up. I love sports and I'm a really fast runner, so sports day is my favourite school day of the year. Unfortunately, it's always held in summer so my allergies try to ruin the fun! My hay fever sets off my asthma, which makes it hard to run. Luckily, I always carry my inhaler and my mum gives me an antihistamine to help stop the hay fever symptoms. Even with my allergies I still came first place in the 100-metre race this year!

If you have asthma, you can still play sports as long as your asthma is well-managed, like Madeline's. Staying active, doing sports and working out can help you stay fit, maintain a healthy weight, and strengthen the muscles in your lungs to help them work better. Make sure you start slowly and keep your inhaler with you, and make sure that any adults nearby know you have asthma so they can look after you.

LIVING WITH ALLERGIES

Having allergies can be difficult and frustrating at times, but they are treatable. Allergies are simply a collection of symptoms caused by the many parts of your immune system – including white blood cells, histamines and antibodies – all working together to protect you.

All allergy symptoms can be treated, whether they are life-threatening or simply uncomfortable and annoying. From antihistamines and EpiPens to immunotherapy and inhalers, there are lots of ways to relieve allergy symptoms.

Now that you know all about allergies and how they work, having an allergy shouldn't be quite so worrying. People with allergies can live active and healthy lives despite their symptoms. They might simply have to be more careful not to eat certain foods, or come into contact with certain materials. Allergies don't have to stop you from doing all the things you want to.

Having a healthy diet and doing plenty of exercise is the best way to keep your body healthy, whether you have allergies or not. Learning about your allergies and how they affect you can help you understand the best ways to look after your body.

TOP TIPS

TOP TIPS FOR FOOD ALLERGIES

- WHEN YOU GO OUT TO EAT, ALWAYS TELL RESTAURANT STAFF ABOUT YOUR ALLERGIES, SO THEY CAN CHECK YOUR FOOD DOESN'T CONTAIN THINGS YOU ARE ALLERGIC TO.
- ALWAYS REMEMBER TO CHECK WHAT ALLERGENS ARE IN CERTAIN FOODS EVEN IF YOU HAVE EATEN THEM BEFORE, BECAUSE RECIPES AND INGREDIENTS CAN CHANGE.
- AVOID EATING IN PLACES WHERE IT IS LIKELY THAT LOTS OF DIFFERENT FOODS HAVE COME INTO CONTACT WITH EACH OTHER, LIKE BUFFETS AND BAKERIES.

TOP TIPS FOR MOULD, DUST MITE AND PET ALLERGIES

- KEEP YOUR HOUSE DRY BY OPENING THE WINDOWS REGULARLY.
- AVOID DAMP BUILDINGS, AND DAMP OUTDOOR THINGS LIKE ROTTEN LEAVES, CUT GRASS AND COMPOST HEAPS.
- WASH YOUR BED SHEETS AND VACUUM REGULARLY.
- WASH YOUR HANDS AND FACE AFTER VISITING SOMEONE WHO HAS A DOG OR CAT.

GLOSSARY

allergist	a doctor who is specially trained in treating allergies
blood pressure	the pressure of the blood in the blood vessels
cells	the basic units that make up all living things
chemicals	substances that materials are made from
constricts	makes narrower
dander	flakes of skin in an animal's fur
digest	to break down food into things that can be absorbed and used by the body
fluid	a substance that flows, especially a liquid
hormone	a chemical in your body that tells cells what to do
immunity	when you cannot be damaged by a certain virus, germ, poison or toxin
ingest	to eat or absorb
inherited	passed down from a parent
microscopic particles	extremely small pieces of a substance that can only be seen with an instrument called a microscope
mucus	a slimy substance that helps to protect certain parts of the human body
proteins	a nutrient found in food which is made up of many amino acids joined together
severe	(of something bad) serious, very great or intense
substance	things with physical properties
swell	becoming larger and rounder in size
symptoms	things that happen in the body suggesting that there is a disease or disorder
venom	a harmful substance that is injected through a bite or a sting
vulnerable	exposed to the possibility of being attacked or harmed

INDEX

Image Credits
All images are courtesy of Shutterstock.com, unless otherwise specified. With thanks to Getty Images, Thinkstock Photo and iStockphoto.
Front Cover, 2 – wavebreakmedia. 4&5 – Konstantin Faraktinov, Satirus, Mega Pixel, Halfbottle. 6&7 – Alex Cofaru, royaltystockphoto.com. 8&9 – goa novi, Fedorov Ivan Sergeevich, wavebreakmedia, Bo Valentino. 10&11 – kitpong sarakot, nobeastsofierce, all_about_people, TouchingPixel. 12&13 – wavebreakmedia, govindji, Aksenova Natalya. 14&15 – Timmar, amperespy44, Vodoleyka, Coprid, JIANG HONGYAN, Hong Vo, virtu studio, pathdoc, NaturalBox. 16&17 – Africa Studio, wilaiwan jantra, LADO. 18&19 – Sudowoodo, Fernando Kazuo, Amy Kerkemeyer. 20&21 – Rob Byron, sciencepics. 22&23 – irin-k, Blend Images, didesign021. 24&25 – LOVE YOU, Yuriy Koronovskiy, Levent Konuk, Davizro Photography, Goncharov_Artem. 26&27 – Sebastian Kaulitzki, pen kanya, ANURAK PONGPATIMET, Lorimer Images, Tatiana Popova. 28&29 – nobeastsofierce, cloki, Subbotina Anna, Leonard Zhukovsky, MediaGroup_BestForYou, Apollofoto, sirtravelalot. 30 – TanyaRozhnovskaya.